DISCOVERING SCOTTISH PLANTS

Edinburgh : HMSO
Royal Botanic Garden Edinburgh
National Museums of Scotland

WHERE TO FIND PLANTS IN SCOTLAND

Plants can be seen anywhere in Scotland. Even people who live in the middle of a very busy city can find plants growing somewhere. Look for mosses and ivy growing on walls, weeds such as fireweed and *Buddleja* (the butterfly bush) springing up on waste ground, and ragwort and dandelions growing in cracks in pavements.

In city parks and gardens all kinds of trees and flowers that have been introduced from abroad

Butterfly Bush   Ivy   Fireweed

can be seen. In the glasshouses of parks and botanic gardens, such as those in Edinburgh, Glasgow, Dundee and Aberdeen, there are tropical plants and examples of rainforest and desert plants to see without even leaving Scotland. In botanic gardens plant names are written in Latin. This is so that botanists (people who study plants) from anywhere in the world know that they are talking about the same plant – common names for plants vary from country to country.

Ragwort

Dandelion

City
Moss, Ivy, Fireweed
Butterfly Bush
Ragwort
Dandelion

Scottish wild plants grow in different habitats. People living near the coast will know the seaside plants that grow on sand dunes, rocks and cliffs – thrift, marram grass, and sea buckthorn etc. Those living in the country will recognise hedgerow and woodland plants – primroses, wood anemones, wild roses and foxgloves. If on holiday in the Scottish Highlands and the west coast, look out for heather moorland plants – bog myrtle, cotton grass, tormentil and cushions of sphagnum moss. On the Scottish hills, moss campion and purple saxifrage may be found growing near the summits, and sundew and butterwort growing in wet and boggy ground.

Wherever you are in Scotland, it is fascinating to find out about wild plants by discovering what they are and how they live.

Marram Grass

Seaside
Thrift, Marram Grass
Sea Buckthorn
Hedgerow/Woodland
Primrose, Wild Rose
Wood Anemone,
Foxglove

Thrift

Sea Buckthorn

Moss Campion

Butterwort

Purple Saxifrage

Foxglove

Heather/Moorland
Cotton Grass
Sphagnum Moss
Scottish Hills
Moss Campion
Purple Saxifrage
Butterwort

Wild Rose

Cotton Grass

Tormentil

FLOWERING PLANTS

A flowering plant is made up of four different parts – the **roots**, **stem**, **leaves** and **flowers** – and each has a special purpose.

The **roots** grow underground and anchor the plant firmly to the earth, although their main purpose is to take in water and food from the soil. Water and minerals (the plant's food) are absorbed through tiny fragile root hairs, and are drawn up through the stem to the leaves and flowers.

The **stem** grows above ground and supports the plant's leaves and flowers. It holds the leaves in the best way for each leaf to get a good share of sunlight, and also carries water up from the plant's roots.

A plant's **leaves** can be **simple** (made up of just one part) or **compound** (divided into many parts). Some leaves are smooth around the edge, and some are notched and toothed. The most important purpose of the leaves is to make food, such as sugars and starches, for the plant. The green colour in leaves comes from **chlorophyll**, which is able to collect energy from the sun and use it, along with water and air, to make sugars.

Petal

Sepal

Stem

Stigma

Stamen

Ovary

Leaf

Roots

The bright colours of many **flowers**, as well as their perfumes, entice insects to visit them and drink their **nectar** (a sweet sticky liquid). Flowers make sure that insects cannot reach the nectar without getting covered in pollen (which looks like yellow dust) from the **stamens**. When the insect visits the next flower of the same kind, some pollen is rubbed off on to the **stigma** Here it grows a tube down inside the **style** eventually reaching the **ovules** in the **ovary** and forming new seeds which, when ripe, are dispersed by wind, water, birds or animals.

Flowers not only use 'tricks' like colours and smells, but also have some others which help protect their pollen. Some flowers close up when it rains, so that the pollen does not get washed away, others hang down their bell-shaped heads, and some even keep their stamens tightly wrapped up until such time as a heavy insect lands on the flower and the stamens pop out.

Annual plants grow from seed, flower and make new seed all in one year. **Biennial** plants grow from seed in the first year and flower, set seed and die in the second. **Perennial** plants grow, flower and set seed every year for many years.

SPRING IN SCOTLAND

Spring usually arrives later in Scotland than in the rest of the British Isles. Seed in packets that state 'plant in March' are often more suited to planting in April or even May. But eventually, the frosts disappear, the days lengthen and everything starts to grow again.

The first sign of spring is snowdrops, although the first native Scottish plants announcing the arrival of spring are hazel and birch trees with their 'lamb's tail' catkins in February. These are covered in yellow dust-like pollen and are the male flowers of the trees. As they depend on the wind to blow their pollen on to female flowers, they appear before the leaves, which would get in the way. Willow trees also have catkins, the most familiar being 'pussy' willows. Later come celandines, violets, primroses, wood anemones, wood sorrel and blackthorn, until suddenly there seems to be a profusion of spring flowers everywhere.

In March look for the little red 'roses' on larch trees. These are the female flowers which later on in the year turn into small brown cones. The larch is the only common cone-bearing tree (conifer) to lose its needles in winter, and in spring its new soft, bright-green needles are very beautiful.

Snowdrop

Celandine

Wood Anemone

Larch Roses

Catkins

Primrose

Wood Sorrel

Look at the shapes and colours of new leaves uncurling and listen to the bird-song as birds busily start nesting. Can you discover which bird produces which song? Stand still and close your eyes. How many different sounds of spring can you hear?

How many signs of spring can you see in this picture?

WHAT TO LOOK FOR IN SPRING

The catkins of willow trees look a bit like soft grey kittens and so we call them 'pussy' willows. Bees are attracted by the nectar they produce and in their travels transfer pollen to other willow flowers.

Coltsfoot is one of the earliest spring flowers and is related to the dandelion. Its leaves look a bit like the shape of a horse's hoof and this is how it gets its name. Its botanical name is *Tussilago* from the Latin word for 'cough', because for a long time the plant was used in cough medicine.

When the blackthorn bush is covered in clusters of white flowers in spring, 'whitethorn' would be a more appropriate name. It is also called sloe. There is a legend about two very poor and ragged children – a brother and sister – who loved playing with the winter snow as they had no toys. When the Queen of the Flowers saw how sad they were when the snow disappeared in spring, she waved her magic wand and suddenly the blackthorn was covered in starry white snow-like blossoms to delight them instead.

Butterbur is an early spring flower which grows by river banks. The pale-pink 'tower' of flowers is one of the earliest sources of nectar for the first spring insects. Later on the huge felt-like leaves appear. In the days before fridges, butter was wrapped in them to keep it fresh. The leaves also make very good sun hats.

The saying 'Ne'er cast a cloot 'til May be oot' – in other words don't cast off your winter woollies too soon – probably refers to hawthorn or May blossom rather than the month of May. In Scotland it is still considered unlucky to bring May blossom indoors, but the tree itself growing in your garden will protect your home from being struck by lightning. The thorns were once used as dressmaker's pins.

Hawthorn

Everyone has made a daisy chain, but how many know that the word 'daisy' in old English means 'eye of the day'? They do look a bit like yellow eyes framed with white 'lashes' and also open in the morning and close at night. Find out what time they open and what time in the evening they close. Do they ever close at other times? Why? Each daisy is really a bunch of many tiny individual flowers on one stem. Spring has arrived when you can place your foot over seven daisies.

Spring
'Pussy' Willow
Coltsfoot
Blackthorn Bush,
Butterbur,
Daisy
Hawthorn

Nature Crafts in Spring

Sowing seeds – outdoors

Spring is the time to plant seeds, but wait until
the frosts are past. Prepare the ground by digging
and raking the earth. The soil must be fine and
not lumpy. Make straight lines using a string line
and the edge of a hoe and sprinkle the seeds
along the row making sure they are not too close
together. The seed packet will tell you how deeply
and how far apart to plant. Gently rake the soil
over the seeds and press it down with the back of
a rake. Don't forget to water the seeds regularly.

Sowing seeds – indoors

Even without a garden, seeds can still be sown in

pots or other containers and kept on the
window sill. Try planting pips from apples and
oranges to grow little trees. Avocado pears will
sometimes grow from the stone – push four pins
into the stone and suspend it over a jar of water
and wait for about six weeks to see if any roots
form. If they do, plant the stone carefully in a
pot. Mustard and cress grow easily on a saucer-
ful of damp cottonwool, tissues or kitchen towel.
Try growing them in an empty egg shell, then
paint a face on the shell and, as the seeds
germinate, watch the mustard and cress 'hair'
gradually grow.

Decorating eggs with grasses, flowers and leaves

This is fun to try at Easter, but ask an adult to help. Hard boil some eggs and leave them to cool. Collect grasses, small leaves and flowers, dip them into cooking oil and then arrange them on the surface of the eggs. Pop the eggs carefully into the toe sections of a pair of old tights, stretching and knotting the tights firmly so that the grasses and flowers are pressed against the material and won't slip. Dye the eggs by boiling them in water with specially-bought non-toxic dyes or use onion skins, tea or beetroot for subtler colours. On removal of the flowers and grasses, their imprint should stand out clearly on the eggs.

11

SUMMER IN SCOTLAND

Suddenly it's summer – and holiday time. In June in the far north of Scotland it is light enough to read a book out of doors at 11pm – if the midges allow. On the Scottish hills during July and August look out for the three different kinds of Scottish heather, as well as starry yellow tormentil and the slender gentian-blue milkwort.

If travelling through northern Scotland on holiday look out for native Scots pine woodland – remnants of the old Caledonian Forest, which once covered parts of Highland Scotland. Now there are only patches left, mainly in Deeside and Speyside (the foothills of the Cairngorms), Glen Affric and parts of Wester Ross. Blaeberries often grow under the trees in Scots pine forest. They are refreshing to eat and make good jam. Also look for foxgloves in the woods and bog myrtle and cotton grass growing in the wetter moorland areas.

Milkwort

Heather

Tormentil

Scots Pine

Queen Anne's Lace

Purple Vetch

Honeysuckle

Roadside verges in summer are full of colour and scent. Look for the frothy flowers of Queen Anne's lace, pink, rambling wild roses (and also the little sweet-scented white 'Jacobite Rose'), honeysuckle, purple vetch and the tall white daisies called gowans. Poppies make a bright-red patchwork in disturbed ground and fields.

Scottish Primrose

The rare Scottish primrose grows in Caithness, Sutherland and Orkney, flowering in July. This beautiful little plant, like the whitebeams on the Isle of Arran, grows nowhere else in the world – these two plants are said to be 'endemic'.

Thrift

Scots Lovage

At the seaside, thrift grows on grassy banks, pale-blue Scottish bluebells, scented purple thyme, white sea campion and cheerful yellow silverweed grow among the sand dunes, and roseroot and Scots lovage on the cliffs.

Bluebell

Roseroot

Sea Campion

Gowans

13

What to look for in Summer – Hills and Moorlands

In England Scottish bluebells are called harebells and in Scotland English bluebells are known as wild hyacinths. Bluebells are found growing on dry grassland, moorland and sand dunes and they flower from July until September. Scottish Bluebell matches have a picture of a bluebell on the box cover and the flower is mentioned in many Scottish songs.

Lady's bedstraw flowers from July to August, and grows on grassy hillsides, machair and sand dunes throughout Scotland. Its dried flowers smell of new-mown hay and were once used to scent linen. The roots produce a bright-red dye and were once used by Highlanders in dyeing wool and cloth. It has been suggested that clan tartans are the colours that they are today because of the dye plants that were available where each clan originated.

There are three types of Scottish heather. Bell heather is the first to flower (as early as July) and has the biggest flowers which are a deep reddish-purple. Ling is the plant that most people mean when they talk of Scottish heather.

Lady's Bedstraw

Scottish Bluebell

Bell Heather

In August and September it turns Scottish hillsides and moorland into a purple-pink haze. Crofters used heather as thatch for roofs, as a dye plant and to make mattresses and brooms, as well as rope (the stems). Heather ale, flavoured with the flowers, was once a popular drink. Cross-leaved heath, with its pale-pink flowers, can be found between July and September. It has much smaller flowers, greyish leaves (rather than green) and the whole plant is covered in soft hairs – bell heather is hairless.

The thistle, with its prickly 'jaggy' leaves, is the floral emblem of Scotland. Its motto is 'nemo me impune lacessit', or 'Wha daur meddle wi' me'. This means that no one attacks a thistle and gets away unharmed. Legend tells us that the emblem was adopted after a surprise night raid by the Danes on Scotland's army failed when one of the attackers trod, barefoot, on a thistle in the dark and let out such a yell that the Scots were alerted and the people saved.

Thyme is a plant often smelt before it is seen – the scent is said to give courage. As a dried herb it can be used in cooking, as well as being added to other flowers to make a pot-pourri. It grows on sandy heaths and in short dry grassland. Bees love it.

WHAT TO LOOK FOR IN SUMMER – ROADSIDES AND SEASHORES

Look at an old 'threepenny bit' coin. Some of them have a picture of a plant of thrift on the back. This is a pun on the word 'thrift' – to save up the coins was said to be 'thrifty'. Thrift, or sea pink as it is also called, is found on rocks and grassy areas at the seaside, as well as high up on the Scottish hills.

Found by roadsides and sand dunes from June to August, silverweed is easily recognised by its bright yellow flowers and silky silvery leaves. Carvings of the flowers are sometimes seen in churches. It is also called 'midsummer silver', and 'goose grey' (because geese like to eat the leaves), and in the past 'traveller's ease' because foot-weary travellers lined their boots with its soft cool leaves.

Thrift

Silverweed

Selfheal

Gowan

Sillar Shakles

Throughout the summer self heal can be found flowering in grasslands as well as open spaces in woods. It was once used to heal wounds. Another name for it is 'carpenter's herb' because carpenters used to grow it near their workshops in case of damaged fingers.

Gowan is the Scottish name for the big ox-eye daisy commonly seen on the roadside verges in July and August. The flower is also called 'dog daisy', 'moon daisy' or, more unusually, 'thunder daisy' – the last because a bunch hanging in your home is said to protect it from being struck by lightning.

Sillar shakles is the Scottish name, once common in Perthshire for quaking grass. The beautiful little heart-shaped silver seed heads of this grass tremble at the slightest touch and quiver in the most gentle breeze:

> *The sillar shakle wags its pow*
> *Upon the brae my deary*
> *The Zephyr round the wunnelstrae*
> *Is whistling never weary*

Nature Crafts in Summer

Pot-pourri

Use lavender flowers, sweet-scented herbs, such as rosemary, lemon balm, scented geranium leaves and eau-de-Cologne mint etc, as well as rose petals to make pot-pourri. Hang lavender stalks in an airy place to dry, then rub off the flowers. Dry bunches of herbs in the same way. Collect red rose petals on a dry sunny day and spread them out to dry on a tray on a sunny window ledge until the petals feel like cornflakes.

Plantain Popgun

Mix scented flowers together adding a little salt and some orris powder (dried root of an iris plant). This should be available in chemist and herbalist shops. Store the pot-pourri in an airtight tin for several weeks before use, giving it a shake occasionally.

Painted pots

Terracotta clay pots can be bought quite cheaply – or perhaps there are some old ones in the garden shed. These can be turned into attractive gifts by painting on a design with acrylic paints. For the best results keep patterns simple and colours bold. Don't get paint on clothes as it is very hard to remove.

Plantain popguns

This game has been a favourite for many generations. Bend the stalk of a plantain over in a loop behind its 'head'. Grasp firmly and slide the loop quickly up to the head to pop it off. At the same time you can chant 'Mary Queen of Scots got her head chopped off.'

Pressed flower pictures

One way to enjoy summer flowers all year round is to press them. Select flowers and arrange them carefully (not touching each other) inside folded sheets of newspaper, placed so that the petals and leaves are flat and put the sheets between heavy books. After about a week check to see if they are dry. The petals will feel brittle when they are, so handle with care. They can then be arranged on coloured card to make cards, bookmarks, calendars, pictures or gift tags. Stick the flowers down with a tiny bit of glue and cover carefully with clear sticky-backed plastic film.

JULY

1 2 3 4 5 6 7
8 9 10 11 12 13 14
15 16 17 18 19 20 21
22 23 24 25 26 27 28
29 30 31

GLUE

STICKY
BACKED
FILM

HAPPY
BIRTHDAY!

PLANT-HUNTING GAME

A counters and dice game for two to four players, showing many of the difficulties faced by past plant hunters. The winner is the first to get on the ship home by throwing the exact number.

Himalayas

OOPS!

Start

you drop plant specimen in a ravine, miss a turn

you find a short cut, go forward 3

you find a rare plant, go again!

good camping place, go forward 2

no bridge across river, miss a turn

you have to get a mule across the river, miss a turn

Scottish Plant Hunters – 1

Scotland has been home to many famous plant hunters who have brought back, from foreign countries, plants that now grow in many of our parks and gardens. Here are the stories of some of them.

Hudson Bay

Canada

Sunflower

Lupin

David Douglas (1799–1834) was born at Scone near Perth. When he was 11 years old he started training as a gardener at Scone Palace, then moved to Culross in Fife before eventually working at Glasgow Botanic Garden. Here he met William Hooker, a famous botanist, who encouraged Douglas to become a plant hunter. Douglas went to the eastern United States, the Rockies and Hudson Bay, collecting and sending home many plants, including lupins, sunflowers and evening primrose. While plant-hunting in the Hawaiian islands he accidentally fell into a deep pit and was trampled to death by a trapped bull. His small dog was later found sitting by the edge of the pit guarding a bundle which contained Douglas's telescope, now kept at the Botanic Garden in Edinburgh. The Douglas fir tree is named after him.

Archibald Menzies (1754–1842) was born in Aberfeldy and gained a degree in medicine at Edinburgh. He travelled as ship's surgeon on the *Discovery* on its round-the-world voyage. At a dinner party in Valparaiso in South America, he was served nuts as a dessert. Instead of eating them he planted them in pots and grew them on the ship's homeward journey round Cape Horn. They were monkey puzzle nuts and this is how monkey puzzle trees first arrived in Britain.

South America

Valparaiso

Cape Horn

Monkey Puzzle Tree

Africa

Asia

Himalayas

Madras

South African Heath

Deodar Cedar

William Roxburgh (1756–1815) was born at Craigie in Ayrshire. He travelled to Madras in India and later was in charge of Calcutta's Botanic Garden. He hunted plants in the Himalayas and was the first person to find the Deodar cedar, which he named. He is buried in Boswell's tomb in Greyfriars Kirkyard in Edinburgh.

Frances Masson (1741–1806) was born in Aberdeen and was chosen to join Captain Cook on his second voyage round the world. He brought back many kinds of South African heaths, which are now grown in many botanic gardens.

Robert Fortune (1812–1880) was born at Kelloe, Berwickshire, became a gardener at the Royal Botanic Garden in Edinburgh and went on to work at the Horticultural Society's garden at Chiswick, London. He hunted plants in China for 19 years and brought back winter flowering jasmine and Dutchman's breeks, both of which are now well-known plants in gardens.

Primula

Rhododendron

Jasmine

Dutchman's Breeks

George Forrest (1873–1932) was born in Falkirk. He also worked at the Royal Botanic Garden in Edinburgh and collected in China. He went on eight expeditions between 1904 and 1930 and brought back over 300 new rhododendrons and more than 50 species of primula. He had lots of exciting adventures while collecting, including fleeing from Tibetan lamas after most of his friends had been killed. Before reaching safety he ate only 'two dozen ears of wheat and a handful of peas' which someone had dropped. One day he had to wade upstream waist-deep in water for a mile to escape his enemies and on another he was shot at by poisoned arrows, two of which passed through his hat.

China

Tibet

Bhutan

Blue Poppy

George Sherriff (1898–1967) was born at Carronvale, Stirlingshire. He worked in a British Mission in Tibet and hunted plants with his friend Frank Ludlow in many areas of Tibet and Bhutan between 1933 and 1949. He too collected many new species of primula and was one of the first plant collectors to bring plants home by aeroplane – much quicker and easier than by ship. He and his wife built a lovely Himalayan garden at Ascreavie in Angus.

Colonel F. M. Bailey (1880–1970) was born in Lahore, India (now Pakistan) but lived most of his life in Edinburgh. He collected plants in many remote areas of Tibet and was the first person to discover the blue poppy, which was later re-found by another famous collector, Frank Kingdon-Ward, who brought it back to Britain. Blue poppies are now planted in many parks and gardens.

Nowadays, plant-hunting is much easier than it was in the 1700s and 1800s. Every year botanists from botanic gardens travel to remote areas of the world and bring back plants for study. New plants are still being found which may prove useful as medicines or food, or which we may eventually grow in our gardens simply to enjoy and admire.

AUTUMN IN SCOTLAND

From September onwards, the weather changes and becomes cooler as the days gradually shorten and darkness falls earlier. There are usually some beautiful autumn days in Scotland which are bright and crisp and full of the colours of autumn leaves – reds, golds and yellows.

Rowan

Acorns

Bramble

Old Man's Beard

Misty mornings leave hedgerows sparkling with raindrops and early frosts glisten on cobwebs. All the fruits of the year, such as red rosehips, rowan and hawthorn berries, purple brambles, crab apples, as well as all the seeds and nuts (hazelnuts, beech nuts, acorns, ash keys and horse chestnuts) can now be seen. The feathery seeds of Old Man's Beard may be seen floating in the breeze, and squirrels rush about gathering nuts and burying them for their winter stores. This is the time to see toadstools in the woods too. Swallows that have been around since April gather in flocks, twittering on telegraph wires, ready to return to warmer countries as insects become scarce and their food source fails. Listen for the cry of the wild geese overhead and look up to see their V-formations as they too fly south for the winter. As gardeners tidy up their plots, the smell of woodsmoke hangs in the air.

How many signs of autumn can you find in this picture?

Can you find a leaf with two, three or even four colours. Try making a leaf rainbow of red, orange and yellow leaves. Gather 10 fallen leaves from the same tree. Choose one and look at it carefully. Now mix them up and see how quickly you can find your leaf again. How did you know it?

Horse Chestnut

Blue Tit

Beech

Rosehip

Hawthorn

Toadstool

27

NATURE CRAFTS IN AUTUMN

Alder cone candle ring

Using a clear, strong glue, stick eight alder cones, end to end, together in a circle. This is fiddly so find a friend to help. Stick tiny dried flowers, tiny pieces of holly or other decorations in the gaps where the cones are joined. The ring should be just the right size to fit round the base of a candle in its holder, but remember the candle ring is not fireproof, so never let the candle burn too far down or leave it unattended.

Leaf rubbings

Choose some autumn leaves with clear vein patterns and place them, lower side up, under a sheet of paper. Carefully rub over the paper with a wax crayon and the shapes of the leaves will gradually appear. You can use different coloured wax crayons and cut out the leaf shapes to make into cards and calendars by sticking them on to a contrasting colour of card.

Bulbs in pots

If you would like spring bulbs flowering indoors on Christmas Day, plant them in September. Soak the bulb fibre overnight and squeeze out any extra water before you line your pots with it. Use attractive, fairly deep containers. You can get specially prepared hyacinth bulbs for indoor planting or you could try miniature iris, tulips, daffodils and crocuses. Leave the tops of the bulbs just above the surface and keep them in a cool, airy place. By about the end of November there should be an inch or two of green showing and the containers should now be brought out into a cool light room. Don't forget to keep the fibre moist, but not soaking wet.

Make a seed tree

Collect as many different seeds, nuts and small cones as you can – acorns, beech nuts, beech mast, alder cones, ash keys and sycamore seeds. Cut out, in cardboard, the outline shape of a tree and use a strong transparent glue to stick your seed collection all over it. Cover the tree trunk with small pieces of bark and add dried lichen round the base to look like grass. This makes an unusual wall decoration.

Winter in Scotland

Winter brings with it short days and long dark nights in Scotland, and sometimes snow as well. On the west coast the surrounding sea, with the warm currents of the Gulf Stream, keeps the temperature higher than in the east.

Winter is the time of year to enjoy tree silhouettes. The leaves have mostly fallen from the deciduous trees now and their different shapes can be clearly seen. It is fun to try to recognise trees without their leaves. Look at the different bark patterns too.

Evergreen trees like the Scots pine are also very obvious in winter and it is easy to find their cones lying on the ground after a windy night. Now is a good time to look at the non-flowering plants (mosses, lichens and ferns) too.

On snowy days bird and animal prints can be seen and followed to find out what has been in the garden or park. Birds are hungry in winter. If you have a bird table, put out wild bird seed to attract different kinds of birds. Remember to also give them water, as puddles and ponds may be iced over.

Look out for frost, which makes patterns on fallen leaves and sparkles on the stalks and seed capsules of many long-gone summer flowers.

WHAT TO LOOK FOR IN WINTER

Holly is used in our Christmas celebrations. The red berries are said to keep away evil spirits and protect our homes throughout the festival. Its berries are slightly poisonous. Holly leaves which are white around the edge and green in the centre are called 'variegated'.

Mistletoe

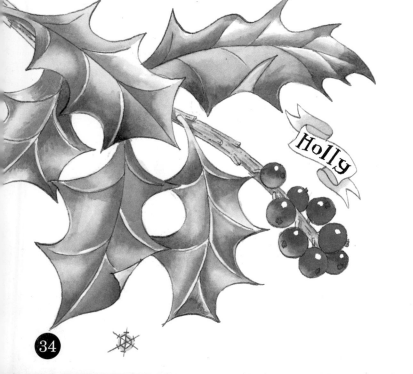

Holly

Mistletoe is a parasitic plant – living on and taking food from another plant. The white gluey berries are spread by birds. Their beaks get very sticky when they try to eat the berries and when they try to clean them by rubbing them hard on a branch of a tree, the seed inside the berry sometimes lodges in a crack in the bark and a new mistletoe plant can grow from it. Mistletoe has long been regarded as a sacred and magical plant, as it is still green and growing when the tree it lives on looks dead in winter.

Yew is another evergreen tree and it has very poisonous leaves and seeds. Each dark poisonous seed is surrounded by a red fleshy cup or 'aril'. Legend tells us that long ago every town grew a certain number of yew trees for the wood which was used to make bows and arrows to defend the towns. For safety they chose to grow them in kirkyards, which were always surrounded by a wall, and this is why we often still see them in churchyards today. There is a very famous yew at Fortingall in Perthshire said to date from pre-Christian times and another, thought to be over a thousand years old, growing on an estate at Whittinghame near Haddington in East Lothian. Here a tunnel has been cut through to enable people to walk in to the centre trunk of the tree.

Yew

Scots Pine

Winter
Holly
Mistletoe
Yew
Scots Pine

The evergreen Scots pine is known as the King of the Woods – the silver birch being the Queen. It is our only native pine tree and near the top of the trunk the bark is a distinctive pinkish-brown colour. As the needles are joined in pairs it is called a 'two-needle' pine. The tall straight trunks were used to make ships' masts and telegraph poles, and turpentine can be made from its resin.

Nature Crafts in Winter

Pine cone bird feeder

Find a large pine cone which is fully open. Wind a piece of florist's wire round the base of the cone leaving a long end for hanging it up when it is finished. Carefully spread smooth peanut butter, preferably unsalted, into all the cracks and crevices of the cone both outside and inside. Now dip the peanut butter-covered cone carefully into a bag of wild bird seed so that the seed sticks all over the cone. The bird feeder is now ready to hang up. Watch the bluetits and other birds enjoying their feast.

Bark rubbings

Winter is a good time to see the trunks of trees clearly and it is fun to make a collection of bark rubbings. Find some white paper, sticky tape and wax crayons. Stick the paper on to the bark of the chosen tree and rub over it carefully with a wax crayon. Gradually the pattern of the bark will appear. Different kinds of trees have different bark patterns. Try to identify a tree just from its bark.

Skeleton leaf cards

Hunt under piles of old leaves to find some that are just skeletons – ones where the soft parts have rotted away leaving just the fine tracery of veins. Take care when handling them as they are very fragile. When you find a perfect one, place it on sticky-backed plastic and put coloured card on top. Try it out first with odd scraps of leaf.

Pine cone carol singers

Find three big pine cones and three table tennis balls.
Draw faces and hair with felt-tipped pens on the balls (or
add wool hair). Carefully pierce holes in the bases of the
'heads' and push over the top ends of the cones which sit
on the broader base. If they wobble, stick a little piece of
blu-tac underneath to hold them steady. Wind
pipe-cleaner 'arms' round the cone, hiding
some of the pipe cleaner under the bracts at
the back. Position the arms at the front to
hold a little carol sheet (which can be made
out of coloured paper). Group the figures as if
they are singing together and make little
paper lanterns for them to hold – attach these
with florist's wire to the hands.

FERNS, MOSSES AND LICHENS

Although winter is a good time to study ferns, mosses and lichens, all of which have no flowers, they can be seen all year round. Ferns have dust-like spores instead of seed. You will find the little spore sacs (sori) on the undersides of the fronds. Mosses also have spores but keep theirs in little heads called 'capsules'. Lichens are really two plants growing together – a fungus and an alga (the simplest kind of green plant).

Here are some common ferns, mosses and lichens to look for.

Hard Fern

Bracken

Hard fern is found all over Scotland on moorland, mountainsides, woods and riverbanks. The fronds feel quite hard and are arranged like the teeth of a comb.

One of the most common ferns found on Scottish mountains, in woods and hedgerows everywhere, is bracken. In winter the fronds wither and are a tawny-red colour. In the past crofters used it as bedding for their cattle and, when burnt, its ashes were used by glass and soap makers. Part of its botanical name is *'aquilina'*, which means 'little eagle', because the inside of a cut stem looks a bit like an eagle with outstretched wings.

Reindeer moss is called moss but is really a lichen. It is found in the moorlands and mountains of Scotland and in the Arctic, where it is common, it is eaten by reindeer and caribou.

Silver Moss

Reindeer Moss

Star Moss

Silver moss is found on waste ground, walls, roofs and in between paving slabs. It grows in tightly packed little silvery-green mounds.

Cup lichen, or pixie cup, is common on walls and rocks in dry places and looks like tiny grey-green cups – just the right size for pixies.

Cup Lichen

Star moss is commonly found on wet heaths, bogs, moorland and by woodland streams. It grows in large 'cushions' and when you look down on it, it looks like a mass of little green stars. Mattresses were once stuffed with star moss.

Crottle is a common lichen found on rocks, trees and walls and for hundreds of years has been gathered as a dye plant to dye wool a deep reddish-brown colour. Traditionally, it is one of the dyes used in making Harris tweed.

There are several kinds of sphagnum moss, all very common on Scottish heather moors and boggy ground. They vary in colour from bright green to orange, pink and red, and form dense soggy mats as they soak up water. Because sphagnum absorbs so well, the Inuit peoples (Eskimos) used it for babies' nappies. It was also used as a wound dressing. Peat is formed from its dead stems and leaves.

Crottle

Sphagnum Moss

Places to Visit

1 **Royal Botanic Garden Edinburgh**

2 **Younger Botanic Garden Benmore**, near Dunoon

3 **Logan Botanic Garden**, *near Stranraer*

4 **Dawyck Botanic Garden, near Peebles**

5 **Glasgow Botanic Garden**

6 **Dundee Botanic Garden**

7 **Aberdeen Winter Gardens**

8 **Inverewe Garden**, Wester Ross

9 **Aberlady Bay Nature Reserve**, East Lothian

10 **St Abbs Head Nature Reserve**, Berwickshire

11 **Scone**, Perthshire – where David Douglas worked as a boy (also exhibition and collection of trees introduced by Douglas)

12 **Caithness, Sutherland and Orkney** – where the Scottish primrose grows

13 **Isle of Arran** – where the Arran whitebeams grow

14 **Fortingall**, Perthshire – where there is a famous yew tree

15 **Whittinghame**, near Haddington – another famous yew tree. (Contact the Earl of Balfour in advance if you would like to visit.)